# A NOTE TO PARENTS ABOUT TEASING

"Sticks and stone can hurt my bones, but names can never harm me." Wrong! Verbal insults can hurt—sometimes more than physical assaults. While teasing may be funny to the person who is slinging the barbs, it is seldom funny to the person who is being teased.

The purpose of this book is to teach children how teasing, when done with the wrong motives, in the wrong place or at the wrong time, can be destructive. In addition, it teaches children how to protect themselves from unwanted teasing.

Reading and discussing this book with your child can motivate him or her to avoid teasing others. It may also help your child feel better if he or she is being teased.

Since teasing is a form of verbal abuse, it cannot hurt if it is not heard. Therefore, the best defense against teasing is to walk away so it will not be heard. If your child is in a situation in which he or she cannot walk away from constant, unwanted teasing, it may be necessary for you to remove your child from that environment. Unfortunately, sometimes teasing can cause long-lasting damage. Therefore, the challenge of avoiding potentially destructive teasing must be taken seriously.

**This book belongs to:**

_____

Published by Scholastic Inc.
90 Old Sherman Turnpike, Danbury, CT 06816.

SCHOLASTIC and associated logos are trademarks and/or
registered trademarks of Scholastic Inc.

ISBN 0-7172-8580-4

First Scholastic Printing, September 2005

# A Book About
# Teasing

by
**Joy Berry**

## SCHOLASTIC INC.

New York   Toronto   London   Auckland   Sydney
Mexico City   New Delhi   Hong Kong   Buenos Aires

This book is about T. J. and his sister, Tami.

Reading about T. J. and Tami can help you understand and deal with **teasing**.

People are teasing you when they annoy
you or make fun of you in playful ways.

Has anyone ever teased you about the way you *look*?

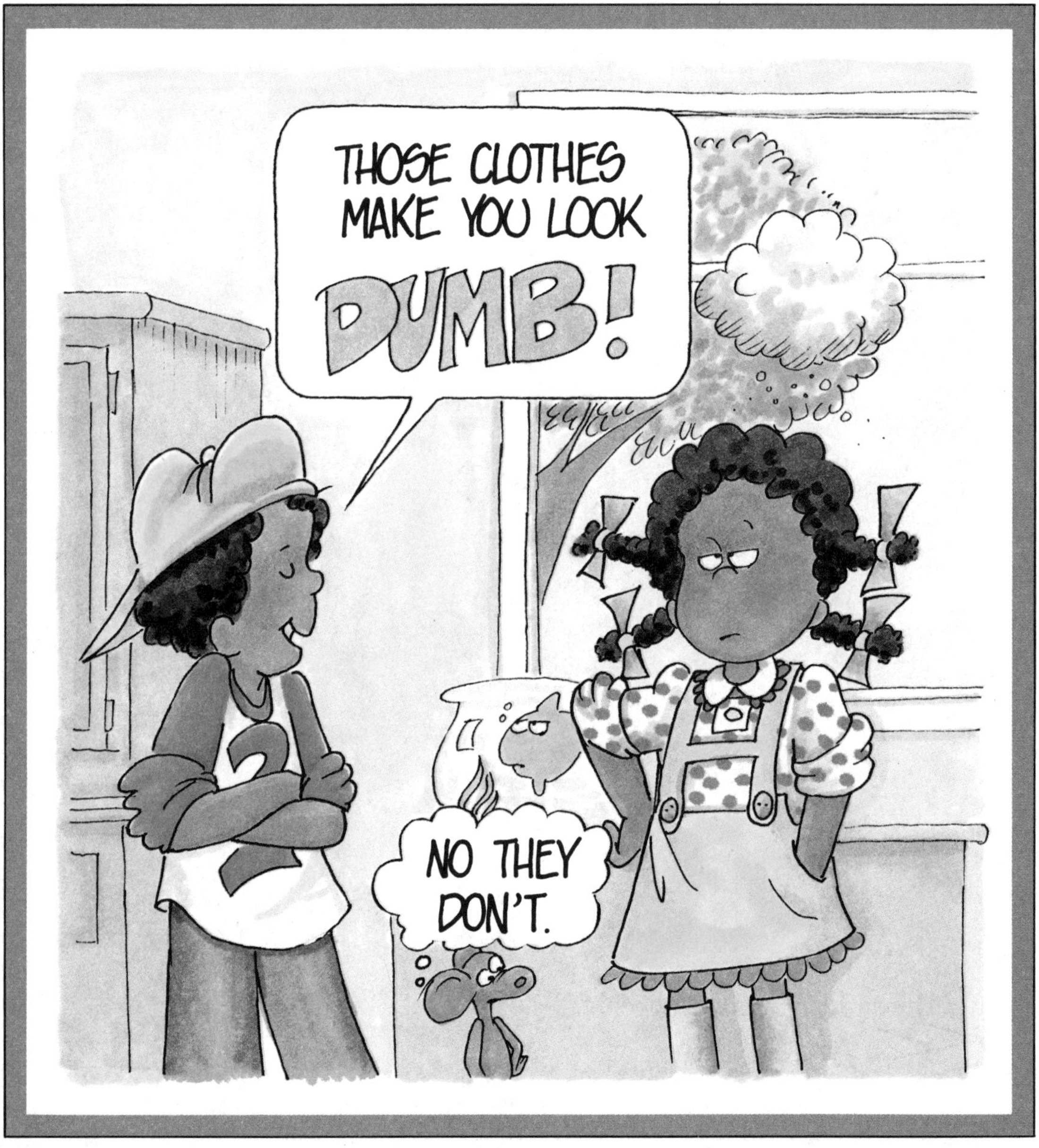
THOSE CLOTHES MAKE YOU LOOK DUMB!
NO THEY DON'T.

Has anyone ever teased you about the way you *think* and *feel*?

Has anyone ever teased you about what you *say* or *do*?

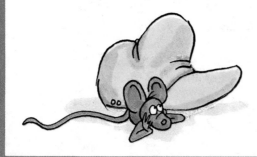

Has anyone ever teased you about what you *like* and *do not like*?

When someone teases you, you might feel frustrated and embarrassed.

You might get upset and become angry.

People who tease often enjoy frustrating and embarrassing others.

They enjoy upsetting others.

Thus, you encourage them to continue teasing you when you become frustrated, embarrassed, or upset.

Do not become frustrated, embarrassed, or upset if you want someone who is teasing you to stop.

Do these things instead:
- Ignore anyone who teases you.
- Walk away from the person if you cannot ignore him or her.
- Do not stay around anyone who continues to tease you.

It is important to treat others the way you want to be treated.

If you do not like being teased, you should not tease others.

Try not to tease.

Do not discuss another person's private thoughts or feelings unless you have the person's permission to do so.

Try not to tease.

Do not say embarrassing things about anyone in front of others.

Try not to tease.

Avoid saying things that might hurt
someone else's feelings.

This is a good rule to follow:
*If you cannot say something nice about someone, avoid saying anything at all.*

If you follow this rule, you will avoid hurting other people's feelings.

It is important to treat other people the way you want to be treated.

If you do not want to be teased, you should not tease others.